Landscape Designer

Helen Mason

Gareth Stevens
PUBLISHING

Please visit our website, **www.garethstevens.com**. For a free color catalog of all our high-quality books, call toll free 1-800-542-2595 or fax 1-877-542-2596.

Library of Congress Cataloging-in-Publication Data

Mason, Helen.
Landscape designer / by Helen Mason.
p. cm. — (Creative careers)
Includes index.
ISBN 978-1-4824-1338-0 (pbk.)
ISBN 978-1-4824-1301-4 (6-pack)
ISBN 978-1-4824-1448-6 (library binding)
1. Landscape design — Juvenile literature. I. Mason, Helen, 1950-. II. Title.
SB473.M37 2015
712—d23

First Edition

Published in 2015 by
Gareth Stevens Publishing
111 East 14th Street, Suite 349
New York, NY 10003

Developed and produced for Gareth Stevens Publishing by BlueApple*Works* Inc.
Editor: Marcia Abramson
Art Director: Melissa McClellan
Designer: Joshua Avramson

Photo Credits: Dreamstime: © Barbara Helgason title p.; © Flashon Studio p. 4; © Barbara Helgason p. 7; © 18042011e p. 8 top; © Colette6 p. 8; © R. Gino Santa Maria / Shutterfree, Llc p. 9; © Andre Nantel p. 10; © Rcavalleri p. 11; © Photoroller p. 12; © Joanne Zh p. 13; © Arne9001 p. 14 top; © Photographerlondon p. 14, 23; © Pavel Parmenov p. 15; © Jodiejohnson p. 17; © Christina Richards p. 19; © Nyul p. 22 top; © Zstockphotos p. 22 bottom; © Brian Goodman p. 26 top; © Beaucroft p. 27; © Lisa Ewing p. 28; © Carlos Neto p. 29 top; © Antonina Vincent p. 31; © Boulanger Sandrine p. 32; © Americanspirit p. 33 top; © Yunhao Zhang p. 35 top; © Monkey Business Images p. 35; © Gavril Margittai p. 36 top; © Radekdrewek p. 36; © Stephen Vanhorn p. 38 top; © Mailis Laos p. 39; © Jerryway p. 40 top; © Jorge Salcedo p. 40; © Jim Parkin p. 41; © Chuongy p. 42; © Linqong p. 43 top; © Vitmark p. 43; © Tannjuska p. 44; © Darkop p. 45; © Helen Mason p. 30; iStock: © skynesher p. 37;© JphilipG. p. 41 top; Public Domain: p. 40 middle, 42 top; Shutterstock: © ChrisMilesPhoto cover; © Wilm Ihlenfeld cover top right; © 2009fotofriends cover bottom left; © Gianna Stadelmyer cover top left, TOC background; © Darryl Brooks cover bottom right; © wavebreakmedia TOC, p. 34; © jesadaphorn yellow note paper; © Dhoxax p. 4 bottom; © Antonina Potapenko p. 5; © Andresr p. 6 top; © Sahani Photography p. 6; © Joe Dejvice p. 9 background; © karamysh p. 12 top, 24; © Robynrg p. 16; © rSnapshotPhotos p. 18 top; © ruzanna p. 18; © Ingrid Balabanova p. 20 top; © cappi thompson p. 20; © stephen rudolph p. 21 left; © Christina Richards p. 21 right; © Elena Elisseeva p. 24 top; © Scott E. Feuer p. 25 top; © MaxyM p. 25; © Darren Baker p. 26; © pics721 p. 29; © spirit of america p. 33 bottom; © jl661227 p. 38 bottom; © Layland Masuda p. 44 top; © USDA. p. 27 top.

Manufactured in the United States of America

CPSIA compliance information: Batch #CS15GS. For further information contact Gareth Stevens, New York, New York at 1-800-542-2595.

Contents

What Is a Landscape Designer?	4
Types of Landscape Designers	6
Landscape Architects at Work	8
Municipal Landscape Design	10
Residential and Commercial	12
Nursery Work	14
Design-Build Firms	16
Working for Yourself	18
Related Careers	20
The Work	22
Drawings	24
Drafting Tools	26
Kinds of Projects	28
A Day in the Life of a Landscape Designer	30
How to Become a Landscape Designer	32
Education	34
Internship Programs	36
Design Portfolio	38
Learning from the Masters	40
How Landscaping Has Evolved	42
You Can Be a Landscape Designer	44
Glossary	46
For More Information	47
Index	48

What Is a Landscape Designer?

Do you like the outdoors? Do you enjoy drawing plans for outdoor areas? Do you like working with your hands? If you answered yes to any of these questions, you might enjoy being a landscape designer.

Landscape refers to the visible features of a piece of land. Landscape designers plan how to make that piece of land the most beautiful and useful it can be.

Landscape designers start by looking at the site as a whole.

- How large is it?
- What is the soil like?
- How is the site being used?
- Where do people enter and exit?
- What pathways exist?

They then develop a plan.

▲ *Landscape designers plan and create gardens that make the best possible use of the land and space.*

4

The Plan

A landscape plan divides an outdoor space into useful spaces and provides an overall look for the site. Yards may have a garden area, a patio, and a small pond. Parks may include a picnic area, a playground, and a water park.

Some plans include a whole neighborhood or city! Whatever the size of the plan, it must consider how the plants will grow and what the area will look like in the future.

▼ Designs include plans for small spaces, such as how best to use an urban backyard.

Types of Landscape Designers

A person who designs landscapes is a landscape designer. Some landscape designers are landscape architects.

Landscape Architects

Landscape architects have a degree in landscape. They have a different and much broader education than landscape designers. In order to get a license, they need to work with an experienced landscape architect. They then take an exam that shows they have the skills they need.

▲ These students have completed their degree in landscape architecture.

▼ Landscape architects produce garden designs, such as the one used for this Japanese garden.

Other Landscape Designers

Landscape gardeners and professional landscapers produce garden designs. They figure out how many plants a site needs. They decide on the particular type of plant to use and how much it will cost. They also advise on how to improve garden soil. They work on outdoor living spaces and garden plans for various types of gardens.

Master gardeners have taken college courses in horticulture. This is the study of how to grow and take care of plants. Master gardeners create gardens, research the needs of different plants, and may give talks on gardening.

Other garden designers work at nurseries and greenhouses where plants are grown. They sketch designs and help clients choose which plants, outdoor furniture, and irrigation systems to buy. For more complicated projects, they might hire landscape architects to help with the areas that they will not or cannot do.

▼ Some community gardens, such as the one pictured here, produce crops for a local food bank.

Landscape Architects at Work

Landscape architects work on large projects, such as school and hospital grounds, conservation areas, and roadsides.

Planning and Designing

▲ Green roofs lower the amount of runoff during storms. They also help to cool the surrounding area.

Landscape architects help people to use, enjoy, and preserve property. They develop and implement plans for conservation and recreational areas.

Developing new ways to promote environmental awareness is part of a landscape architect's job. They encourage the use of green **infrastructure**. This is the use of nature to cool buildings and help water drain away from them. Roof gardens contain layers of soil and plants. These green roofs absorb rainwater and make pleasant green spaces.

▼ Landscape architects who work for a city are also responsible for the safety of playgrounds.

Supervising

Landscape architects take charge of large projects that can be regional or even super-regional in size. They manage landscape workers and sometimes also supervise engineers, other architects, and planners.

They check finished work. They must ask themselves: Does it follow the plan? Is it well done?

Landscape architects work with the government to evaluate landscape plans. They may suggest improvements. They also help to restore and maintain historical and cultural sites, such as parks and gardens.

▼ Landscape architects are managers. They supervise other professionals and landscaping crews.

Municipal Landscape Design

Municipal landscape designers work for city and regional governments on many different projects.

Landscape Design and Care

Municipal landscape designers design and care for public spaces. These include roads, parks, beaches, trails, and buildings.

City streets look better if they have trees and flowers. Government buildings and parks are more appealing with grass, trees, and gardens. These are all planned by designers. So are hiking paths and bicycle trails.

Designers plan and take care of fitness trails. They also landscape the ground around libraries and airports. Sometimes they make a plan for an entire region.

▼ *This street design includes trees and flowers that can withstand dry conditions.*

New Construction

Landscape designers plan new picnic and dog park shelters, park lighting, and wading pools. They keep costs within a **budget**. This can involve shopping around for good deals on materials.

Special Needs

Landscape designers know safety and **accessibility** are vital. People in wheelchairs must be able to get into public buildings. Playgrounds for children must have safe equipment and ground covering.

Some parks have special trails, playgrounds, and even sports fields that have been designed for handicapped users.

◀ A former US Coast Guard facility in New York Harbor is being turned into an 87-acre park and public space known as Governors Island Park.

Residential and Commercial

Landscape designers work on both residential and commercial sites.

Residential Landscape Design

Residential sites are places where people live. These can be small urban lots or large rural properties.

Residential projects include gardens, patios, and swimming pools. Designers make an overall plan for each area. They plan walkways, patios, and fencing.

▲ In dry Arizona, landscape designers must create gardens that don't need much water.

◀ Swimming pool areas are among the projects that landscape designers work on.

Commercial Landscape Design

Commercial landscape designers work on business and government spaces. These include company headquarters, hospitals, parks, zoos, and **condominiums**.

If the building is new, landscape designers may plan the complete landscape. They decide how to level the land and where to leave a slope. They also decide where to put trees, bushes, and gardens.

If the site is old, they may update the landscaping. This can include putting in solar lighting.

Some sites have been changed or damaged by the way they were used in the past. Landscape designers look for ways to restore the land when the site is updated.

▶ Landscape designers planned the pool and plantings for this condominium.

13

Nursery Work

Because most nurseries are small, nursery landscapers do many different jobs. They use hand and garden tools to plant, care for, and transplant trees and other plants. They sell and deliver plants to customers. They may also take care of the greenhouse and operate both indoor and outdoor watering systems. They keep their work area clean and take care of the grounds around the nursery.

Nursery landscapers also help the sales team to design landscapes. Some also take care of the plant library.

▲ *This worker inspects plants for insects and disease.*

◀ *This nursery landscaper answers questions about the type of climate and amount of water needed by various plants.*

Work for Customers

These kinds of landscapers may help to build projects designed for a customer. They water, weed, trim, and fertilize customer properties.

They create new gardens by planting seeds, flowers, and trees. In the spring, they plant annuals, which are plants that last one year. In the fall, they prepare **perennials** for winter. They may also lay grass sod.

During holiday seasons, nursery workers may create special displays for homes and businesses.

▼ *Heavy machinery is used to transplant trees such as this one.*

Design-Build Firms

Many people hire a designer to help plan their landscaping. Once the design is finalized, they find a **contractor** to do the work. Design-build firms both design plans and build landscape projects.

Design and Build

Design-build firms have architects, designers, and construction workers. One or more architects will work with landscape designers to develop plans. They buy the needed stone, plants, lumber, and other materials. The plans and materials go to a construction supervisor. Construction includes preparing the site, digging holes, building everything needed, leveling the land, and planting.

The design-build firm then puts in all the finishing touches, such as signs and decorations.

▼ *The design for this Las Vegas garden considered Nevada's dry climate.*

Nature-Friendly Approach

Some design-build firms focus on creating sustainable site plans. These use fewer natural resources and do little harm to the environment. Native grasses are a key part of some designs. There are good reasons to use plants that grow naturally in an area. Native plants are already adapted to the climate and soil conditions. They are more resistant to local diseases and pests than plants imported from somewhere else.

Advantages

Design-build firms use a collaborative process where everyone works together. This provides a smooth transition from idea to plan to construction. It can also mean lower costs and a faster finishing time. Another advantage of design-build firms is having the same person responsible for all aspects of the job.

▼ *Native plants and pebbles replace grass in this sustainable site plan.*

Working for Yourself

Freelance landscape designers are hired and paid by the job.

Variety of Work

These landscape designers plan simple landscapes for private customers. In many cases, they also build the project. Then they work throughout the year to take

▲ *A landscaping truck can be used to plow snow in the winter.*

care of the plantings. Some also do pool care. This includes removing the pool cover, cleaning and vacuuming the pool area, and keeping the water at the correct level, temperature, and chemical balance.

In the winter, some landscapers plow driveways. They may also build garden furniture and start young plants.

▼ *This landscape freelancer is taking care of his client's pool.*

Hazard Protection

Landscape designers wear protective gear to keep safe. Long sleeves and pants reduce the amount of skin exposed to the sun and hazards such as poison ivy. Safety goggles, gloves, and steel-toed boots protect eyes, hands, and feet. Earplugs prevent hearing damage.

Truck Office

For many freelancers, their truck is their office, where they keep their daily schedule, garden plans, and bill books. The truck also carries their many tools. Power tools include mowers, various trimmers, and a leaf blower. Hand tools include clippers, shovels, garden forks, rakes, hoes, pruning tools, and a wheelbarrow.

◀ This freelancer's truck is used for tool storage and as an office. It is also used to transport materials such as this load of **mulch**.

Related Careers

Many careers and jobs are related to landscape design.

Landscape Technician

Landscape technicians take care of plants, bushes, and trees. They design and put in new gardens, walkways, and retaining walls. They treat plant

▲ *This landscape technician is laying sod for a new lawn.*

diseases and do everything they can to keep plants strong and healthy. They care for the **golf greens** on golf courses. This includes fertilizing, mowing, and spraying herbicides or weed killers. Some take care of motorized equipment.

Other landscape technicians care for the grass at baseball and football stadiums. They are called groundskeepers.

▼ *This landscape technician is driving a tractor to mow the grass on a golf green.*

Tree Care

Arborists are tree specialists. They plant, take care of, and cut down trees. Some work with highway crews and utility companies to clear fallen trees after a storm.

Stone Work

Stonemasons work with different types of stone. They use hammers, mallets, air drills, and chisels to shape rocks. They use these to build stone walls and floors.

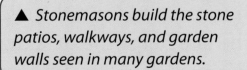

▲ *Stonemasons build the stone patios, walkways, and garden walls seen in many gardens.*

◄ *This arborist is removing branches to keep this tree healthy.*

The Work

The landscaping design process begins with listening to what a client wants and balancing that with what the site can handle.

Starting the Plan

Landscape professionals must ask themselves the following questions:

What does the client want? Is privacy important? Is the design for a single person or a young family? What are the plans for the future? What is the site like? How large is it? Where does the sun hit at various times of the day? Is there a lot of wind? What is the rainfall pattern?

Information from the client and the site helps the designer make the original plan. This will suggest design elements such as patios, walkways, and fencing. It also includes the type, size, and color of plants.

▲ This landscape designer meets with a client to assess the site and hear what the client wants.

▲ The use of evergreens means this front entrance will look stylish year-round.

Location

Each landscaping plan considers the location. People in hot areas need shade plants, while people in windy areas may need a wind block. The slope of the land and how well it's drained can also affect both the plants used and the plans for the area.

Cost

The price for each part is included in the plan. The plan answers any question a customer may have including: How much will each part cost? What is the overall price? How much of this is for materials? How much is for the designer?

Usually, there is a fee before the work starts. The customer pays a certain amount while the work is being done. There is a final payment once everything is finished.

▼ The plants in this garden are beautiful, even in dry conditions. Gardens like this are ideal for dry states such as California.

Drawings

Once the client and the designer have come to a basic agreement, the designer moves to the next step of drawing a full plan. All the details will be finalized in the plan. These include selection of plants, design of stairs and walkways, and use of lighting fixtures. Detailed landscape plans provide a bird's-eye view of the property and allow the client and the designer to determine whether one projected component will interfere with another.

▲ *Well-designed steps provide a safe way to get up and down this steep slope.*

▼ *Well-placed light sources are important additions to a proper landscape design plan.*

Working Drawings

With the client's okay, the designer makes a working drawing or scale drawing of the site. This shows the property boundaries, the location of all buildings, and each part of the design.

Using this drawing, the designer checks the cost and availability of plants and materials. The designer also contacts the local government about any necessary permits.

The designer then carefully goes over the drawing with the client to make sure that all is done to his satisfaction.

▲ This working drawing is for a garden and walkway beside an urban home.

▼ Spruce trees can survive cold winter temperatures.

Drafting Tools

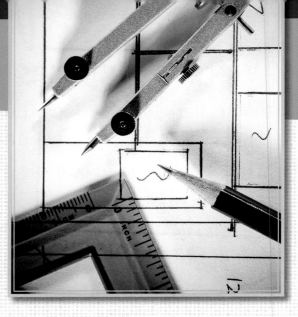

All designers need **drafting tools**. Software tools and plant manuals also help.

Software Design Tools

There are a number of software programs for landscape design. Some allow designers to drag and drop features onto pre-made

▲ *Landscape designers start with basic drafting tools.*

landscape **templates**. They can see the design in both two and three dimensions. They can also share or print designs and even link them to photos and suppliers.

Simple programs include *DynaSCAPE*, *SketchUp*, and *SmartDraw*. *CS Artisan, Realtime Landscaping Architect, LANDWorksCAD, PRO Landscape, VizTerra, Virtual Property Architect™*, and *EARTHSCAPES* are more complex.

▼ *Before buying, wise landscape designers check the reviews of various landscape design software packages.*

Other Tools

Garden planning can also be done on paper or using software. Check online for inexpensive garden planning software.

USDA Plant Hardiness Zone Maps show average annual minimum winter temperatures. Each zone is separated by 10°F. Landscapers use these maps to decide which plants to grow in a particular area.

Plant manuals are available in print and online. There is information on the best location for each plant, how much water it needs, and most common diseases.

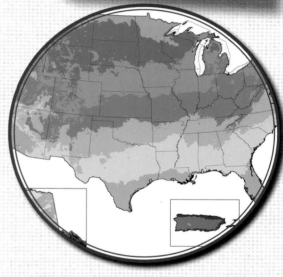

▲ Plant Hardiness Zone Maps are available from the US Department of Agriculture.

▼ There is a wide range of plant manuals, including ones for fruit, landscape and nut trees, plants with berries, flowering plants, and vegetables.

IC GARDEN

N DESIGN

herbaceous borders

THE COTTAGE GARDEN

the perfect Rose Garden

the GARDENER'S HANDBOOK

FLOWERING SHRUBS

G TUBS & POTS

ENER LAWNS

ARDEN WATER FEATURE

ARDEN LANDSCAPING

THE PERFECT Patio Garden

TREES & SHRUBS

the guide to VEGETABLE garden

PLANTS & FLOWER

THE LITTLE BOOK OF GARDEN TI

Kinds of Projects

Landscape designers plan the construction of patios, decks, pools, and spas. They also develop **irrigation** and lighting.

Outdoor Spaces

Landscape designers confer with customers about the location and style of patios and decks. They will ask:

- ❍ What materials does the customer want?
- ❍ Will the deck or patio be in full sun or shaded?
- ❍ Will it have direct access to the house?
- ❍ Will it include cooking facilities?

The designer will suggest a style to suit the house and property. The plan includes ideas for plants, accessories, and seating. Once the client approves a design, the landscaper gets the necessary permits and starts the construction part.

◄ Designers plan the size, shape, and surroundings of backyard ponds.

Other Projects

Many backyards are planned around a swimming pool. Landscape designers suggest the best spot. They design the pool, its deck, and all fencing.

Many pool areas include a spa pool with water jets, a change house, and lighting both in and around the water. Designers plan these. They also suggest the best plants, depending on the climate and amount of sun. Some also plan the style and color for pool furniture.

▼ Designers also plan automatic watering systems for large gardens.

▼ This pool has an irregular shape to make it more interesting. Can you see the fence? The landscape designer has hidden it with trees and shrubs.

29

A Day in the Life of a Landscape Designer

A landscape professional's days are full of variety. They include both office and outdoor work. This is a sample day of a self-employed landscape designer specializing in residential homes.

Indoor Work

An office day starts around 8:30 a.m. The landscape designer researches different looks for a garden. This includes checking online and leafing through a stack of books and magazines. To help with the inspiration, the designer might also go through the photos of finished projects.

▲ *Photos such as these are used in design portfolios, on company websites, and in advertising brochures.*

A new client calls to discuss a potential landscaping job. The designer sets up a meeting to see what the site looks like.

At midday, the designer has a lunch meeting with a new contractor who just started working in the area. The contractor specializes in hardscaping and would like to partner on jobs.

Back in the office, the designer finishes the day by working on planting lists and completing a drawing for a new project.

Outdoor Work

Outdoor work is usually done from spring to fall. Landscape designers drive to the job sites in their trucks. They go to nurseries to buy all the plants required for a job. They supervise the workers they hired to build and plant the garden.

A designer's busy day also may include checking on a finished garden to make sure it is being maintained properly. The designer also visits the tool rental store to discuss the rental fees, and may set up a schedule for renting the machinery for specific jobs, such as big augers needed for planting trees or digging holes for fence posts.

When meeting a new client, landscape designers bring along a sketch pad or notebook for jotting down details and sketching up property measurements. They also bring a portfolio of their previous work. They ask many questions so they can fully understand what the client wants.

▲ Landscape designers sometimes work with exoctic plants to create unique backyards for their clients.

31

How to Become a Landscape Designer

If you are interested in landscape design, you can get started right now.

Begin at Home

Mow and care for your own lawn. Talk to your neighbors. Offer to mow lawns, rake leaves, and help with gardening — for a fee. That's how many landscapers begin! Experiment. Make notes about what you like best and why.

Create a flower or vegetable garden. Buy plants at a nursery, or start seeds indoors and move them to your garden. Research how to care for your plants.

Make a Planter

Consider designing and building a planter. Fill it with plants. In the process, you will learn how to use drafting tools, a little about carpentry, and the needs and care of various plants.

◀ *Build a planter. Fill it with plants that do well in your area.*

Join and Volunteer

Join your school's environment club and volunteer to plant trees. Help with planting, watering, weeding, and picking at a community garden.

Research the outdoor and naturalist clubs in your area. Get involved. Many outdoor groups do hands-on work restoring natural landscapes.

Research the ACE Mentor Program of America, Inc. Through this program, professional designers introduce students to work in design. Find out how you can take part.

When you are old enough, get a part-time job working with a landscaper or at a plant nursery.

▼ These Boy Scouts are doing landscape work at Gettysburg National Military Park.

▶ These teens help restore a section of stream. See what the outdoor and naturalist clubs in your area are doing.

Education

Many landscape designers complete high school. They then have the choice between going to college or university, or learning on the job.

High School

Many high school courses teach skills needed for landscape design.

- ○ Drafting courses teach the use of drafting tools. Some also use drafting software.
- ○ Art provides information on the different effects that colors create.
- ○ An environmental studies course discusses many ways people can help the environment. These include reducing the use of chemical **herbicides** and growing native plants.
- ○ Math classes teach how to calculate square footages, prices, budgets, and other figures that landscape design clients will need to know.
- ○ Computer skills help landscape designers run a business efficiently.

After High School

Some landscape designers are self-taught. These people often work as gardeners or landscape workers part-time during high school. Some intern with landscape designers, architects, contractors, or gardeners.

Universities and community colleges offer degrees and certificates in landscape design and in horticulture. Many universities offer degrees in landscape architecture.

▼ High school field trips can provide an introduction to landscape design.

▲ Many colleges and universities teach courses in landscape design. Check with your school counselor.

Internship Programs

Internships allow people to learn skills as they work. Landscape design internships can be both formal and informal.

Formal Programs

Before getting their license, landscape architects work with a landscape architecture firm after earning their degree. During this period, they receive coaching from experienced architects. At the end, they take the Landscape Architecture Registration Exam (LARE). Passing this exam certifies them as landscape architects.

▲ *These student interns are learning by doing volunteer fieldwork.*

The National Park Service also offers internship programs. At the Olmsted Center for Landscape Preservation, interns work with staff members. Internships usually last six months.

◄ *There are many opportunities with the National Park Service.*

Informal Programs

Many businesses have informal internship programs. For example, many landscaping companies and nurseries hire hard-working young people with an interest in landscape design. They coach trainees on the job. These interns learn how to care for plants and construct landscapes.

Trainees who show interest and ability are allowed to do more. Some start designing projects for the same company.

▼ These interns are learning from hands-on experience. Some will go on to become landscape designers.

Design Portfolio

Lanscape designers have design portfolios to help convince clients to hire them. It can also help to have one to get into design courses.

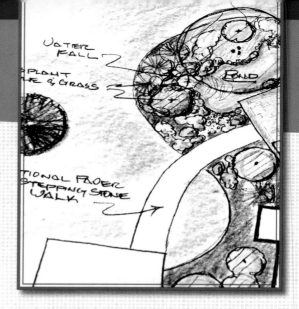

Usual Content

Once you have completed several design projects, try to create your own design portfolio. A design portfolio shows off your experience, talent, skill, and creativity. Start with your name, address, and contact information. Show 10 to 12 projects. Include drawings, plans, and photos of finished work.

Make sure your plans show the location, size, and cost of each project. If you don't use design software, draw the site to scale. Include symbols for various elements and a legend. If you use design software, record the name of the software package.

◄ *The software used for this plan uses full color. It can also produce a three-dimensional version of the plan.*

Special Content

Your portfolio should include additional information that shows how your work is received. Letters of praise from people who are happy with your work make a good impression.

If you have written an article or blog, mention it. Landscape designers include copies of any work in print and URLs for online material.

List all related volunteer work and any awards or certificates. If you are a student or associate member of a professional group, say so.

Your portfolio may start small, but it will grow as you do more projects.

▼ Take photographs of all your garden designs as well as all the flowers you have worked with.

Learning from the Masters

Thomas Chalmers Vint

Thomas Chalmers Vint (1894–1967) shaped the US National Park System. He used native materials such as logs and stones. Because of him, America's parks look natural, even though large numbers of people visit each year. He also suggested wilderness parks. These are isolated areas where few people are allowed.

▲ *Thanks to Thomas Chalmers Vint, America's national parks, such as Mount Rainier National Park, have kept much of their flavor.*

Hideo Sasaki

Hideo Sasaki (1919–2000) believed that landscape could restore the human spirit. This could be done by working with a site's land, buildings, and environment. He taught at Harvard and led a major design firm.

▶ *Sasaki designed Boston's Christian Science Center and its famous reflecting pool.*

Martha Schwartz

Martha Schwartz likes working in plastic and stone. She recycles urban spaces using bright colors, sharp lines, and artificial structures. Her unique gardens often don't have either plants or water. Besides running her own design firm, Schwartz is an author and university professor.

▲ *Martha Schwartz's playful design is seen here in the Jacob Javits Plaza in New York City.*

Janet Meakin Poor

Janet Meakin Poor was 40 when she received a degree in landscape architecture. She has used her knowledge to help endangered species. Working with national and international groups, she collects and preserves seeds from endangered plants. These seeds contain **genetic** material she wants to preserve.

▼ *Some plants grow only after the land has been burned over. Janet Meakin Poor encourages research into how to burn some areas to encourage these plants.*

How Landscaping Has Evolved

Landscape design is based on traditional gardens from around the world.

Early Gardens

There is evidence that gardens existed as early as 3500 BC. Records report that Babylon had roof patios in 600 BC. These patios were irrigated and planted with colorful plants collected in many countries.

In Japan, Zen gardens were enclosed by a wall. Their stones and simple design provided a place to think.

▲ *The Hanging Gardens of Babylon contained flowers and fruits from many countries.*

▼ *The only plant in a Japanese Zen garden is moss. Trees can be seen outside the walls.*

The Greeks and Romans had walled gardens with raised beds. Decorations included statues, stone basins, and marble tables.

Gardens of the Middle Ages

These gardens provided both medicine and food. They were fenced. Plant beds were raised to help with drainage. Gardens often included an orchard and fish ponds. Some castle gardens had mazes. A maze is a tall hedge grown in a complex pattern. People had fun trying to find the way out!

▲ In China, gardens symbolized the universe. Different garden elements represented aspects of nature.

▼ Traditional Greek gardens are enclosed spaces where people can get away from their busy lives.

You Can Be a Landscape Designer

Do you still want to be a landscape designer? Check out the following characteristics. Which traits do you have? Which ones are you developing?

▲ *This student is experimenting with a design program.*

I am

- ❏ artistic
- ❏ good with my hands
- ❏ physically strong
- ❏ organized
- ❏ good with computers

I enjoy

- ❏ creating beautiful spaces
- ❏ working outside
- ❏ collaborating with people

If you have or are developing these traits, you might make a great landscape designer.

▼ *Balconies can be beautiful or boring. Design an eye-catching balcony for your area.*

Set Your Goal

Decide what kind of landscape designer you want to be. Research the needed training either online or by talking to a school counselor. Ask yourself:

○ What schools offer the courses you need?
○ What high school credits do you need?
○ What marks do you need to get into those schools?
○ Where can you intern to get experience?

▲ *Design and build a no-mow yard in a private or public space near you.*

Take Steps Now

Get a job at a nursery or garden store when you are older. Learn everything you can about plants and how to grow them.

Design a balcony garden for an elderly person. Take photographs of how it looks throughout the year. Offer to help neighbors with landscaping projects.

Ask to job shadow a local landscape designer. Take pictures that show a day in the life of that designer. What skills does the designer have? What can you do to develop those skills?

Glossary

accessibility the quality of being reachable or usable

budget a plan that determines how much money can be spent and how it will be spent

condominium dwellings that are grouped together like rental apartments, but they are owned by individual residents.

contractor a person who is hired to do work or to provide goods at a certain price and by a certain time

drafting tools items used for technical drawing, including pens, rulers and often computer programs

focal point center of interest or attention

genetic relating to genes and inherited traits

golf green area of specially prepared grass around the holes on a golf course where putts are played

herbicides chemicals used to destroy plants, especially weeds

infrastructure the basic framework of something, especially used to describe the roads, bridges, and other public works in an area

irrigation watering land by artificial means to help plants grow, such as using pipes to bring in water from far away

mulch a material (often leaves or small pieces of wood) that is spread around plants to protect them and stop weeds from growing

municipal having to do with the government of a city or town

perennial a plant that lives for two years or more, especially small flowering plants that grow in spring and summer, die in the fall, and return in the spring

pervious a word to describe a substance that allows water to pass through it

sod surface layer of ground containing grass and grass roots

template a pattern or mold for something that is being made

For More Information

Books

Foster, Kelleann. *Becoming a Landscape Architect: A Guide to Careers in Design.* Hoboken, NJ.: Wiley, 2009.

Hill, Lewis, and Hill, Nancy. *The Flower Gardener's Bible: A Complete Guide to Colorful Blooms All Season Long.* North Adams, MA: Storey Books, 2003.

Websites

ACE Mentor Program of America, Inc.
www.acementor.org
Learn how you can find someone to help you work toward a career in design.

American Horticultural Society
www.ahs.org
Join the American Horticultural Society and learn about plants.

National Association for Olmsted Parks
www.olmsted.org/naop-about/about
This group works to protect and restore many parks around the US.

Index

A

accessibility 11

ACE Mentor Program
  of America, Inc. 33, 47

arborists 21

B

budget 11, 34

C

collaborative 17

college 7, 34, 35

commercial 12, 13,

community gardens 7, 33

condominium 13

contractor 16, 30, 35

D

decks 28, 29

design-build firms 16, 17

design process 22

design software 26, 38

drafting tools 26, 32, 34

E

environment club 33

F

fee 23, 31, 32

fitness trails 10

focal point 25

G

gardeners 7, 35

golf greens 20

government buildings 10

green roofs 8

H

herbicides 34

horticulture 7, 35

I

infrastructure 8

internships 36, 37

irrigation 7, 21, 28

L

landscape architects 6, 7,
  8, 9, 31, 35, 36

landscape architecture 6,
  9, 35, 36, 41, 43

M

managers 9

mulch 19

municipal 10

N

National Park Service 36

naturalist clubs 33

natural resources 17

nurseries 7, 14, 31, 33, 37, 45

O

Olmsted Center for
  Landscape Preservation
  36

P

parks 5, 9, 10, 11, 13, 40, 43

patio 5, 12, 21, 22, 28, 42

perennials 15

pervious 11

pond 5, 28, 43

pool 11, 12, 13, 18, 28, 29, 40

portfolios 30, 31, 38, 39

property boundaries 25

public spaces 10

R

residential 12, 30

S

stonemasons 21

T

technician 20

templates 26

trees 10, 13, 14, 15, 20, 21,
  25, 27, 29, 31, 33, 42

U

university 34, 41

USDA Plant Hardiness
  Zone 27

V

volunteer 33, 36, 39

Z

Zen gardens 42